AMERICA IN WORDS AND SONG

The Constitution

The Story Behind America's Governing Document

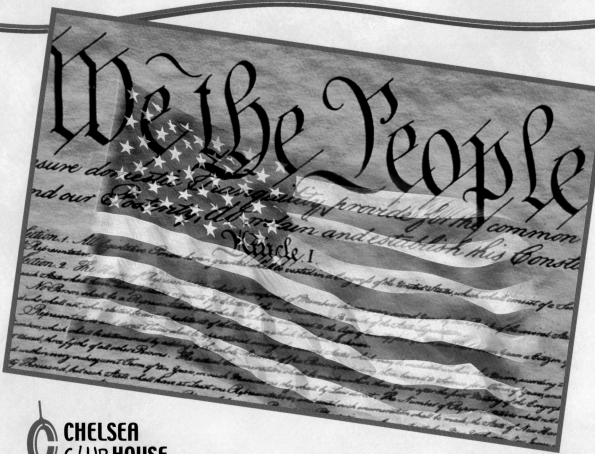

CHELSEA CLUB HOUSE

An Imprint of Chelsea House Publishers

A Haights Cross Communications Company

Philadelphia

Kerry A. Graves

Chelsea Clubhouse books are published by
Chelsea House Publishers, a subsidiary of
Haights Cross Communications Company.

A Haights Cross Communications Company

The Chelsea House World Wide Web address is
www.chelseahouse.com

Printed and bound in the United States of America.

9 8 7 6 5 4 3 2 1

Library of Congress Cataloging-in-Publication Data
Graves, Kerry A.
  The Constitution: the Story Behind America's Governing
Document / by Kerry A. Graves.
    p. cm.— (America in words and song)
Summary: Describes the process of writing the Constitution, how
it became law, what the document means, and how it has kept
the United States government strong as the country has grown
and changed.
Includes bibliographical references and index.
  ISBN 0-7910-7333-5
1. Constitutional law—United States—Juvenile literature.
2. Constitutional history—United States—Juvenile literature.
[1. Constitutional law—United States. 2. Constitutional history—
United States. 3. United States—Politics and government.]
I. Title. II. Series.
KF4550.G73 2004
342.73'02--dc21   2003004038

Selected Sources

Feinberg, Barbara Silberdick. *The Articles of Confederation: the
First Constitution of the United States.* Brookfield, Conn.:
Twenty-First Century Books, 2002.

Kelley, Brent. *James Madison: Father of the Constitution.*
REVOLUTIONARY WAR LEADERS. Philadelphia: Chelsea
House Publishers, 2001.

Nardo, Don. *The U.S. Constitution.* HISTORY OF THE WORLD.
San Diego: KidHaven Press, 2002.

Editorial Credits

Gia Marie Garbinsky, editor; Takeshi Takahashi, designer;
Mary Englar, photo researcher; Keith Trego, layout

Photo Credits

Table of Contents

Introduction

In 1965, teenagers Mary Beth and John Tinker got ready for school. Both wore armbands to protest the Vietnam War. When they arrived at school, they were suspended because school officials thought the armbands were disruptive. The Tinkers thought this was unfair, and they sued the school district.

Their case went to the highest court in America. In 1969, the Supreme Court ruled that the wearing of armbands is a form of free speech protected by the First Amendment to the Constitution, and that it was **unconstitutional** for the school to prevent students from wearing them.

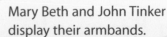

Mary Beth and John Tinker display their armbands.

The First Amendment

An amendment is a change. The **Founding Fathers** expected to make changes to the Constitution. The first change took place in 1791 when ten amendments, called the Bill of Rights, were added. The First Amendment guarantees Americans the right to speak and write freely, to freely practice their religions, to gather in peaceful protest, and to **petition** the government. This amendment protected the Tinker's right to free speech and peaceful protest in 1965—178 years after it was written!

4

The **framers** of the Constitution gathered in 1787 to create a system of government that would unite the American states and give the people power to choose who would govern them. They wanted the Constitution to last. They created "a living document" that could be changed as Americans' needs changed. And, after gaining independence from Great Britain in the **American Revolution**, the framers wanted to create a system that would prevent any one part of the government from becoming too powerful.

They created a democratic republic, a government in which the people elect representatives to express their opinions in Congress.

These were new ideas for the late 1700s. European nations doubted they would work, but they did. The Constitution has guided America for more than 200 years.

The Constitution declares the laws of our nation, the powers and duties of our government, and the rights of Americans. It is the oldest set of governing rules in use by any nation today.

The Articles of Confederation

Most American colonists came from England. They crossed the Atlantic Ocean, and battled the elements and untamed land to build homes and communities. Even though they lived in America, the King of England ruled them from 3,000 miles away. As the years passed, the colonists grew more connected to life in their new country and became less **tolerant** of a king who knew little of America. On April 19, 1775, American colonists stood up to British soldiers, and the American Revolution began.

In May, **delegates** from all of the colonies except Georgia gathered in Philadelphia, Pennsylvania. This gathering was called the Continental Congress. The delegates asked Thomas Jefferson to write the Declaration of Independence.

But declaring independence meant throwing away the laws that had guided them as colonies of Britain. So, the 13 newly independent states desperately needed to form a government that would unify them and help direct the war effort.

Americans ride through Massachusetts, warning Minutemen that British soldiers are coming. Minutemen were American colonists who were ready to fight in "a minute's notice." Minutemen and British soldiers fought the first battle of the American Revolution in Lexington, Massachusetts, on April 19, 1775.

Left to right: Thomas Jefferson, Roger Sherman, Benjamin Franklin, Robert Livingston, and John Adams. These delegates to the Continental Congress formed the ideas in the Declaration of Independence. Jefferson also wrote the Declaration of Independence. Meanwhile, other delegates wrote the Articles of Confederation.

The delegates produced the **Articles of Confederation** to provide rules that would loosely join the states together. It created a congress, or central government, in which each state had one vote. The men who created the Articles knew that because they were fighting a war for independence against a king with too much power, they could not give their own congress much power.

They gave Congress the power to go to war, but not to raise taxes, control trade, or settle problems between states. During the Revolutionary War, the nation worked fairly well under the Articles. But when the war ended in 1783, the states, which were no longer united by a common enemy, stopped working well together. Soon, the weak Congress under the Articles caused problems within the new country.

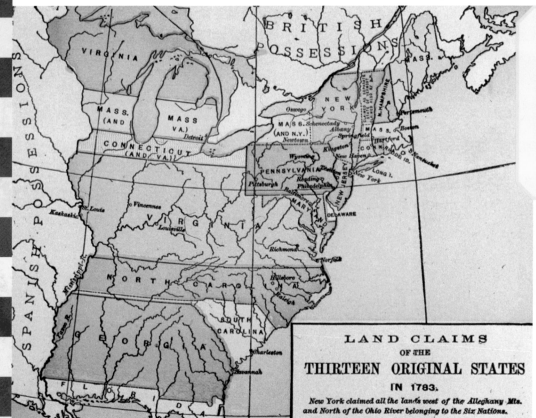

This map shows the land of the 13 original states in 1783. After the Revolution, people thought of themselves as citizens of their states, rather than citizens of America. They called themselves New Yorkers or Virginians, not Americans.

LAND CLAIMS
OF THE
THIRTEEN ORIGINAL STATES
IN 1783.

New York claimed all the lands west of the Alleghany Mts. and North of the Ohio River belonging to the Six Nations.

Within a few years, both Congress and the states had **financial** trouble. The states no longer made money from trade with Great Britain. America had **debts** from the war, but no money to pay them, because Congress could not collect taxes. Each state was supposed to help pay the debt but most paid only part of their share. Congress had no power to make them pay.

Instead each state used the money as it saw fit.

To raise money, the states taxed the products they traded with other states. This led to arguments between states and high prices for everyone.

Farmers who could not pay their bills went to jail. Their farms were sold to pay their bills. People became angry.

In September 1786, 600 armed farmers stormed a local courthouse in Massachusetts. They believed that if they could stop the court from meeting, they could prevent local authorities from taking more farms. The **rebellion**, led by a farmer and former soldier of the American Revolution named Daniel Shays, grew and spread to other states. Soldiers from Massachusetts finally ended Shays' Rebellion on February 3, 1787.

Shays' Rebellion worried some Americans, including George Washington and James Madison. They realized that similar rebellions could happen in other parts of America. They also realized that the United States needed a stronger central government that could prevent further rebellions within the country.

Congress called for a meeting in Philadelphia, where delegates from the 13 states would change the Articles of Confederation. Fifty-five delegates from every state but Rhode Island attended. This gathering of delegates became known as the Constitutional Convention.

A mob blocks a Massachusetts courthouse in 1786. Daniel Shays had been a captain during the Revolution. As one of many farmers in debt after the war, Shays led a group of farmers who rebelled against the courts. This rebellion became known as Shays' Rebellion.

The Constitutional Convention

Delegates to the convention had different opinions on how to change the Articles of Confederation. Some wanted a new document to strengthen the central government. All realized the current system wasn't working well and a change had to be made. Some feared the new nation wouldn't survive.

The delegates had to **compromise** to form a new constitution. Within four days, the Virginia delegates presented ideas for a new government. This became known as the Virginia Plan.

James Madison

James Madison began his career in politics in 1774. He served in the nation's Congress from 1780–1783. In 1787, a 36-year-old Madison suggested that delegates from each state meet in Philadelphia and amend the Articles of Confederation. This meeting became known as the Constitutional Convention.

During the convention Madison's ideas helped to form the Virginia Plan, on which our Constitution is based. Later he became a member of the first House of Representatives, and wrote the first ten amendments to the Constitution, known as the Bill of Rights. Because of the role he played in forming the early American government, he became known as Father of the Constitution.

Even after the Constitution was written, Madison continued to play an important role in America's history. In 1809, he became America's fourth president.

James Madison, Father of the Constitution.

The delegates who gathered to change the Articles of Confederation met in the Pennsylvania State House in Philadelphia. In 1787, Philadelphia was the largest and most modern city in the nation. It was also a central location for the delegates.

The first meeting of the Constitutional Convention was scheduled for May 14, 1787. James Madison, a delegate from Virginia, was the first to arrive on May 3. In the days before the others arrived, Madison studied books on government and wrote his ideas for a brand new American government.

George Washington, also from Virginia, arrived next, on May 13. When he rode into Philadelphia in his horse-drawn carriage, it seemed that all of the city's 40,000 residents lined the streets to see him.

Benjamin Franklin's arrival to the State House was the most interesting of all the delegates. At 81, Franklin, who lived in Philadelphia, had several health problems. Finding it too uncomfortable to be jolted around in a carriage, Franklin had four prisoners from the Philadelphia jail carry him to the State House in a **sedan chair**. This made for a much smoother ride.

Other delegates traveled to Philadelphia on horseback or by **stagecoach**. Heavy rain that spring made for muddy and flooded roads, and many delegates were late to arrive. By May 25, delegates from a select group of seven states had arrived, and the first meeting of the Constitutional Convention took place.

George Washington leads the debate of the Continental Congress. He had become a respected commander of American soldiers during the American Revolution and was unanimously voted president of the convention because of his experience.

The Pennsylvania State House, pictured below, was the location of the Constitutional Convention and the signing of the Declaration of Independence. Today the building is called Independence Hall.

Great Compromise

The Virginia Plan described a **federal** government with an executive branch (president), a judicial branch (court system), and a legislative branch (Congress).

In this plan, the states would be represented in a congress of two houses, the Senate and the House of Representatives. State governments would elect the senators. The people would elect representatives. The number of senators and representatives of each state would depend on the state's **population**.

The Virginia Plan would join the states into a nation under a strong federal government. This shocked delegates who had come to change the Articles of Confederation. They didn't want a strong central government.

Delegates who opposed a strong national government proposed the New Jersey Plan. This plan gave power to the government of each state, not the people. Under the plan, as under the Articles, Congress was a single body in which each state had one vote, but it would gain power to collect taxes and control trade. Instead of a president, several executives, chosen by Congress, would direct the government.

Assembly Room in Independence Hall, where delegates to the convention met. Even though it was hot, delegates kept the windows closed so they could speak freely without outsiders hearing the debates and trying to influence the delegates.

Members of the Constitutional Convention debate the issues.

Delegates from small states tended to like New Jersey's plan. This plan provided each state with one vote in Congress regardless of its population. As a result, all states had the same power. Delegates from states with larger populations tended to like Virginia's plan. In this plan the number of votes a state had in Congress was based on the state's population.

On July 16, delegates adopted The Great Compromise. Congress would consist of two houses, the Senate and the House of Representatives. Each state would have two senators who would be elected by their state governments. The people would elect each state's representatives, and the number of representatives from each state would be based on the state's population.

With this matter decided, the delegates moved on to other issues. What powers would the president, Congress, and the courts have? And how could they guarantee that no one part of the government could become too powerful?

The United States government consists of three branches: the legislative branch (Congress: House of Representatives and Senate), the executive branch (president, vice president, and their departments), and the judicial branch (the courts). The legislative branch makes the law. The executive branch does the work to make it possible for the law to be put into action. And the judicial branch interprets the law.

To guarantee that one branch cannot gain too much power and harm the country, the writers of the Constitution created a system of Checks and Balances. This system gives each branch certain powers, but that power is checked in various ways by the other two branches.

For example, Congress has power to make laws. But the president can refuse to approve the law. Congress can overpower the president's refusal if two-thirds of its members vote to do so. The Supreme Court has power to reject a law that does not agree with the Constitution. The president chooses members of the Supreme Court, but his choices must be approved by the Senate. Also, the president is commander in chief of the military, but only Congress may declare war.

Today, members of Congress—the Senate and the House of Representatives—do their work at the United States Capitol, in Washington, D.C.

The White House has been home to every president except George Washington. Washington chose the site for it. Construction began in 1792. John Adams, the 2nd president, was the first to move in, in 1800.

The delegates debated other issues at the Constitutional Convention, including slavery. Some delegates favored ending slavery. Southern delegates argued that their plantation economy depended on slave labor. In another compromise, the delegates agreed to wait until 1808 to decide the issue of slavery.

Another difficult debate focused on whether to include a bill of rights, a list of the freedoms of individual citizens. The delegates decided against it. Most state governments had a bill of rights to protect their residents, so it seemed unnecessary to have one in the Federal Constitution, too.

Not surprisingly, the delegates also disagreed about how to **elect** the president. Big states with more people wanted the people to elect the president. Smaller states wanted each state's **legislature** to elect the president. The delegates compromised by creating the Electoral College.

Every American citizen who is 18 or older has the right to vote. Here, former President Bill Clinton (with daughter Chelsea) exercises his right to vote in the 1992 presidential election. Clinton won the election and became the 42nd U.S. president.

The Electoral College is a system in which the people vote for their president through other people called electors. Each state has a certain number of electors. The number of its electors is equal to its total number of senators (2), and its total number of representatives (which is based on the state's population). Larger states with larger populations have more electors than smaller states with smaller populations. Today, the **political parties** with **candidates** running for president choose the electors for each state.

Every four years, on Election Day in November, the people of each state vote for president. Their votes are recorded and counted. The candidate who wins the most votes from the people in a state gets all the electors of that state. It is the votes of the electors that count in determining which candidate wins the election.

There are 538 total electoral votes. To become president, a candidate must win more than half of these, or 270 electoral votes. This explains why candidates for president travel from state to state, giving speeches. They are trying to win the election state by state, a handful of electoral votes at a time. A candidate doesn't have to win the most votes in total, just the most votes in enough states to reach 270 electoral votes. And it is possible to win the presidency by winning the most electoral votes but not the most individual votes.

George W. Bush won the 2000 presidential election and become the 43rd U.S. president. He won the election by gaining the most electoral votes, while his opponent, former Vice President Al Gore, won the most individual votes.

Former Vice President Al Gore ran against George W. Bush in the 2000 presidential election.

The Constitution Becomes Law

After four months of debate, the Committee of Style and Arrangement wrote a final draft of the Constitution. Its original first line, "We, the people of the states of North Carolina, Virginia,..." was changed to "We, the people of the United States…" because the new government was one of individuals united as one nation, rather than as citizens of separate states.

Only 42 of the original 55 delegates were still in Philadelphia on September 17, the day the Constitution was signed. Many had left the convention because of disagreements over some of the compromises that were made. When it came time to sign the Constitution, 39 signed and 3 refused. Two of the delegates who refused to sign feared that the people would not like the government created by the Constitution. The third refused because the Constitution did not include a bill of rights.

The Signing of the Constitution.

Next, the document was sent to the 13 states. Newspapers printed it for the people. Debates, like those at the convention, followed in each state's ratification convention. Each state could join the United States under the Constitution or remain independent. But to make the Constitution official, nine states had to accept it.

Many states feared that a strong central government would ignore the rights of individual citizens. Some states agreed to approve the Constitution only if a bill of rights listing the individual freedoms of American citizens was added.

In 1788, New Hampshire became the ninth state to approve the Constitution. Rhode Island was the last state to approve it, in 1790, more than one year after the first Congress and the first president, George Washington, took office.

George Washington officially becomes the first president of the United States of America in New York, in 1789.

The Constitution and Its Meaning

The Constitution is the supreme law that is the design for the United States government. It was created to last long into the future. Every citizen in America, including the president and other members of the government, must follow the rules of the Constitution.

The Constitution has three parts: the Preamble (or introduction), the articles, and 27 amendments that have been added since the original document was written. The words of the Preamble are as follows.

> "We the People of the United States, in Order to form a more perfect Union, establish Justice, insure domestic Tranquility, provide for the common defense, promote the general Welfare, and secure the Blessings of Liberty to ourselves and our Posterity, do ordain and establish this Constitution for the United States of America."

The Preamble explains that the Constitution will declare the laws of the nation, maintain peace inside the country, set up military defenses, and take care of the people of the nation by assuring their freedom and the freedom of Americans in generations to come. The very first words, "We, the People" make it clear that the people will make the decisions about how the government is run.

"[The Constitution] is much to be wondered at…a little short of a miracle."
—George Washington,
1st United States President
1789–1797

The body of the Constitution is made up of seven articles that tell how the government will be organized and what the specific responsibilities of the branches of government are.

Article 1 defines the legislative branch (Congress), the jobs it will perform, and how politicians will be elected to Congress.

Article 2 describes the executive branch (president, vice president, and the other members who the president might appoint) of the government.

Article 3 lists the powers of the judicial branch (the court system). This article also defines which actions of an individual against the country are considered **treason**.

The Supreme Court Building in Washington, D.C. The Supreme Court, the highest court in the nation, heads the judicial branch of the American government.

Article 4 describes relationships among states. It provides that each state will accept other states' public acts, records, and proceedings. It also explains how new states become part of the nation.

Article 5 gives the rules for adding amendments to the Constitution.

Article 6 describes how office holders in the three branches of government are bound by oath to support the Constitution. It also states that no religious test is required to hold a central government office.

Article 7 explains how the Constitution will go into effect after nine states accept it.

A handwritten draft of the Fifteenth Amendment to the Constitution, passed in 1870, which declares that citizens may not be denied the right to vote because of their race. Article 5 of the Constitution allows for amendment to the Constitution.

"Our Constitution works. Our great republic is a government of laws, not of men."
—Gerald R. Ford, 38th United States President, 1974–1977

When the Constitution was debated at the state ratifying conventions, many officials were upset that there was no bill of rights. Most of the ratifying conventions proposed changes to the Constitution. Delegates of each state convention who were expected to be elected to Congress stated their intent to develop amendments and propose them to the states.

The states sent in 90 different ideas for amendments to be part of the Bill of Rights. James Madison was a member of the first House of Representatives in the new Congress, and in June 1789, he proposed that Congress begin working on the Bill of Rights. He became the main author of the ten amendments added to the Constitution in 1791. These first ten amendments are known as the Bill of Rights.

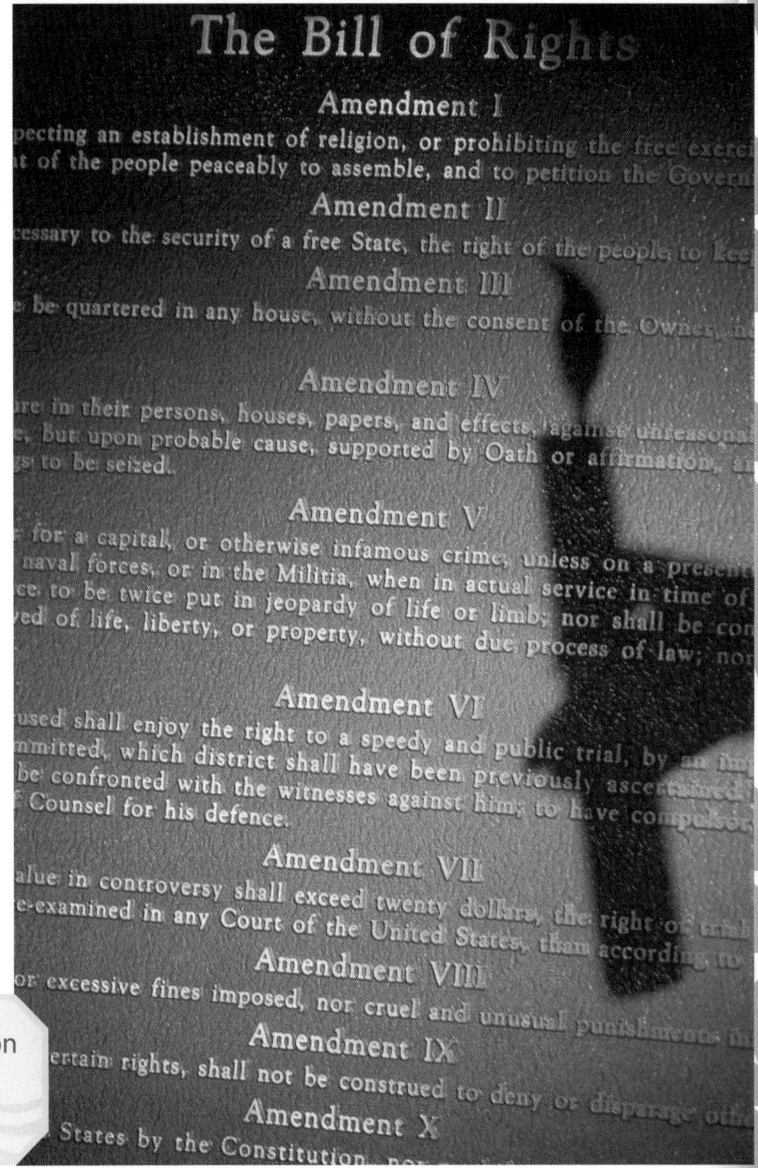

The first ten amendments to the Constitution were added in 1791. They are known as the Bill of Rights, pictured here.

The women marching in this picture are exercising their First Amendment rights to free speech and peaceful protest. The signs they carry express their goal of gaining the right to vote.

The First Amendment guarantees Americans the right to speak and write freely, to freely practice their religions, to gather in peaceful protest, and to petition the government.

The Second Amendment protects Americans' right to own and bear weapons.

The Third Amendment states that the government is not allowed to force citizens to let soldiers stay in their homes. (This happened during the American Revolution.)

The Fourth Amendment requires legal authorities, such as the police, to get written permission from the courts to enter and search citizens' homes.

Amendments Five through Eight state the rights that Americans have in civil cases. These rights include the right to be considered innocent until proven guilty in court, and the right to a trial, a lawyer, and a fair jury.

The Ninth Amendment states that individual rights of the people are protected even if they are not specifically listed in the Bill of Rights.

The Tenth Amendment recognizes that the people will retain all powers that have not been given to the central government or their state government.

Since the addition of the Bill of Rights to the Constitution, 17 more amendments have been added. The Thirteenth Amendment, added in 1865, ends slavery. The Fifteenth Amendment, added in 1870, recognizes African Americans' right to vote. The Nineteenth Amendment, added in 1920, recognizes women's right to vote. The last amendment to the Constitution, the Twenty-seventh Amendment, was added in 1992. It outlines rules for giving pay raises to members of Congress.

Women celebrate the passage of the Nineteenth Amendment to the Constitution in 1920, which gave women the right to vote.

The Constitution Today

The delegates to the Constitutional Convention wrote the Constitution in four months. They knew then that they could not prepare the government for everything that could happen in the future. They knew the United States would change and grow. To allow for change and growth, the delegates included directions for making future changes (amendments) to the Constitution in Article 5.

The delegates were right. America has changed drastically since the Constitution was written. In 1790, about 4 million people lived in America. Now more than 288 million people live in the United States. In addition to the land that made up the original 13 states, millions of square miles have been added to the nation in the form of 37 new states.

Even with all these changes, the Constitution has worked for more than two centuries because it can change and grow.

The United States of America today.

People's lives change every day in response to events that happen in their communities, their states, their nation, and the world. These events shape their opinions about how their government should work. The United States Constitution gives the people power to express these opinions by voting for senators and representatives who share their ideas. These politicians make laws and can propose constitutional amendments that reflect the opinions of the people who elected them.

The men who wrote the Constitution created a system that depends on the people making their voices heard through public elections. Today, every American citizen who is 18 years of age or older has the right to vote. And doing just that is precisely how "We, the People" can "form a more perfect Union."

The Statue of Liberty is a strong and inspiring symbol of the freedom that citizens of America enjoy.

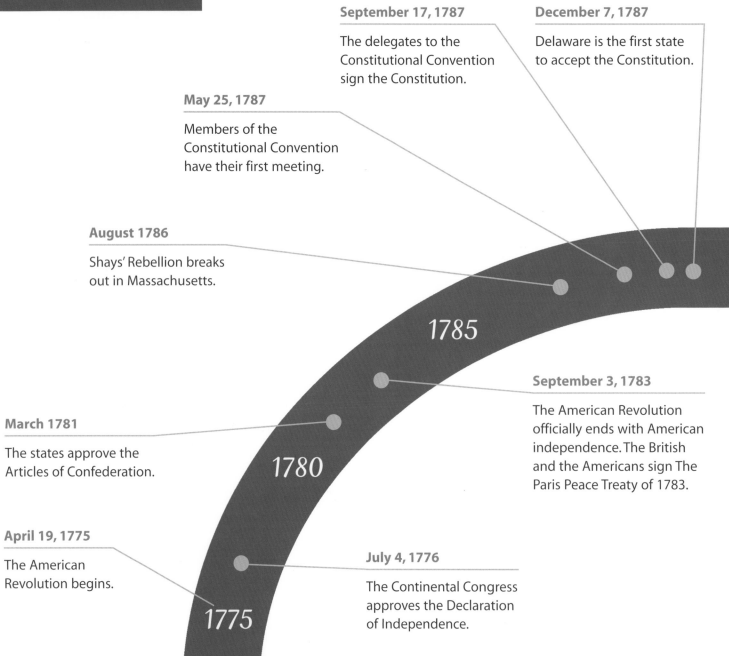

September 17, 1787

The delegates to the Constitutional Convention sign the Constitution.

December 7, 1787

Delaware is the first state to accept the Constitution.

May 25, 1787

Members of the Constitutional Convention have their first meeting.

August 1786

Shays' Rebellion breaks out in Massachusetts.

1785

September 3, 1783

The American Revolution officially ends with American independence. The British and the Americans sign The Paris Peace Treaty of 1783.

March 1781

The states approve the Articles of Confederation.

1780

April 19, 1775

The American Revolution begins.

July 4, 1776

The Continental Congress approves the Declaration of Independence.

1775

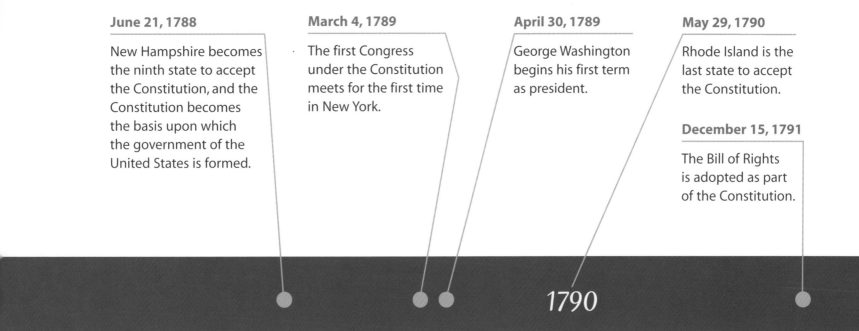

June 21, 1788

New Hampshire becomes the ninth state to accept the Constitution, and the Constitution becomes the basis upon which the government of the United States is formed.

March 4, 1789

The first Congress under the Constitution meets for the first time in New York.

April 30, 1789

George Washington begins his first term as president.

May 29, 1790

Rhode Island is the last state to accept the Constitution.

December 15, 1791

The Bill of Rights is adopted as part of the Constitution.

1790

The World in Colonial Times

While the American colonies were forming an independent government what else was happening in the world?

★ In 1777, Alexander I of Russia is born.

★ British explorer Captain James Cook discovers Hawaii in 1778.

★ James Watt patents a double-acting steam engine in 1782.

★ In 1787, James Madison and Alexander Hamilton begin the publication of *The Federalist Papers*.

★ The French Revolution begins with the storming of the Bastille in 1789.

★ In 1789, Russian explorers found Odessa on the Black Sea.

★ Washington, D.C., is founded in 1790.

Glossary

American Revolution (uh-MER-uh-kuhn rev-uh-LOO-shun) the war in which America won independence from Great Britain

Articles of Confederation (AR-ti-kuhls uhv kuhn-fed-er-AY-shun) the first United States constitution

candidate (KAN-duh-date) one who competes to win a position

compromise (KOM-pruh-mize) to agree to accept something that is not exactly what you wanted

debt (DET) the situation of owing someone money

delegate (DEL-uh-gate) someone who attends a meeting to represent the opinions of other people. Delegates to the Constitutional Convention represented the opinions of the people of their states.

elected (i-LECT-ed) chosen by a vote

federal (FED-ur-uhl) a form of government in which power is shared by a central authority and state governments

financial (FYE-nan-shuhl) relating to money

Founding Fathers (FOUND-ing FAH-thurs) the delegates to the Constitutional Convention of 1787

framers (FRAYM-urs) the delegates to the Constitutional Convention of 1787

legislature (LEJ-iss-lay-chur) refers to a legislative body, or Congress, with power to make laws. A state's legislature is its Congress. Each state has its own Congress that is separate from the Congress of the federal government.

petition (puh-TISH-uhn) to make a formal written request for something you want

political parties (pa-LI-ti-kuhl PAR-tees) organized groups of people who share the same general beliefs about the way the government should be run. The Democratic Party and the Republican Party are two examples.

population (pop-yuh-LAY-shuhn) the total number of people living in an area

rebellion (ri-BEL-yuhn) open and violent resistance to an established government

sedan chair (si-DAN CHAIR) a portable, often covered chair that is fastened to long poles and carried on the shoulders of two or four men

stagecoach (STAYJ-kohch) a carriage pulled by horses

tolerant (TOL-ur-ant) willing to endure or put up with

treason (TREE-zuhn) the crime of betraying your country or attempting to remove its government

unconstitutional (uhn-kon-stuh-TOO-shuh-nuhl) a law or action that disagrees with any idea not authorized by the Constitution

To Learn More

READ THESE BOOKS

Catrow, David. *We the Kids: The Preamble to the Constitution of the United States*. New York: Dial Books for Young Readers, 2002.

Kelley, Brent. *James Madison: Father of the Constitution*. REVOLUTIONARY WAR LEADERS. Philadelphia: Chelsea House Publishers, 2001.

Nardo, Don. *The U.S. Constitution*. HISTORY OF THE WORLD. San Diego: KidHaven Press, 2002.

Quiri, Patricia Ryon. *The Bill of Rights: A True Book*. New York: Children's Press, 1999.

Quiri, Patricia Ryon. *The Constitution: A True Book*. New York: Children's Press, 1999.

LOOK UP THESE INTERNET SITES

Ben's Guide to U.S. Government for Kids

http://bensguide.gpo.gov/index.html

This site provides information for students in kindergarten through 12th grade. A cartoon Benjamin Franklin describes the parts of the United States government, and explains political vocabulary and national symbols. The site includes games and links to other government Websites for kids. The site also includes biographical information about Ben Franklin.

Constitution Society

http://www.constitution.org

This site provides more in depth information about the Constitution.

Independence Hall Association

http://www.ushistory.org/

This site gives information about Independence Hall, where the Constitution was written. It also highlights the Liberty Bell, the Declaration of Independence, the Revolutionary War, and other historical people and places associated with Philadelphia.

James Madison's Montpelier

http://www.montpelier.org

This Website provides information about the Madison family and the history of their estate, Montpelier.

The National Archives Experience

http://www.archives.gov/national_archives_experience/constitution.html

This site provides a wealth of information about American history, including the complete text of the Constitution and information about the men who wrote it.

National Constitution Center

http://www.constitutioncenter.org/

This museum in Philadelphia's Independence National Historical Park features a Website with interactive displays, films, and actors to describe the creation of the Constitution.

INTERNET SEARCH KEY WORDS

The Constitution, Declaration of Independence, Constitutional Convention, Founding Fathers, James Madison, George Washington, American History, Bill of Rights

Index